T0353814

SHIFT WITH SYMBOLS

13 Sacred Symbols
to Create a Peaceful Life

by Lena L. Springer

Copyright © 2024 Lena L. Springer.

All rights reserved. No part of this book may be used or reproduced by any means, graphic, electronic, or mechanical, including photocopying, recording, taping or by any information storage retrieval system without the written permission of the author except in the case of brief quotations embodied in critical articles and reviews.

Balboa Press books may be ordered through booksellers or by contacting:

Balboa Press
A Division of Hay House
1663 Liberty Drive
Bloomington, IN 47403
www.balboapress.com
844-682-1282

Because of the dynamic nature of the Internet, any web addresses or links contained in this book may have changed since publication and may no longer be valid. The views expressed in this work are solely those of the author and do not necessarily reflect the views of the publisher, and the publisher hereby disclaims any responsibility for them.

Any people depicted in stock imagery provided by Getty Images are models, and such images are being used for illustrative purposes only.
Certain stock imagery © Getty Images.

Interior Image Credit: Debora Bogart

ISBN: 979-8-7652-4079-3 (sc)
ISBN: 979-8-7652-4080-9 (e)

Library of Congress Control Number: 2023906078

Print information available on the last page.

Balboa Press rev. date: 02/24/2024

I dedicate this book to
all those who wish to live
in more Peace, Love and Joy.

DISCLAIMER

I am not a doctor and I do not diagnose, treat, or prescribe. These symbols are not meant to cure any disease in the body; they are not a substitute for medical attention or advice; they are simply a guide to help you keep a positive mindset through the difficult times. They are meant to help take your mind off of what does not feel right in your life until you can return to that feel-good space within your heart and your mind.

Table of Contents

Foreword

When Lena first gifted me with the opportunity to read her book in its unfinished form, I was excited and honored. As an author myself, I know the intimacy that exists between a writer and her book. As a guide, teacher and facilitator of healing for the Modern Mystery School, I see not only the value of these pages, but also have witnessed the metamorphosis of the writer as she has become a beautiful, empowered woman.

This is a very special book. It is about the connection between our physical, mental and emotional worlds, and the world of Spirit. It is about helping you, the reader, to move beyond the mundane by engaging your heart in a language that you intuitively already know.

The language of God can be found in signs and symbols. And that is what this book is about – connecting to the Divine through the language of God. How exciting is that?!

I believe that Lena was given these symbols to share with you to help you bridge the gap between the negative ego and the Divinity within you. In meditating on these symbols, you have the opportunity to empty your cup and to become receptive to the messages of the soul, which is the interface of your physical being and your Spirit.

As an added bonus, Lena shares her life experience of moving from a place of insecurity, anxiety and a negative sense of self to the amazing, strong and self-assured person that she is today. Lena has given you tools to navigate some of the pitfalls of life and is generous in her sharing of things that have helped her.

What you have in your hands is a gift. And the fact that it *is* in your hands is no mistake. Make good use of it, and enjoy this taste of the world of Spirit!

Christine Elwart
Guide, Healer and Teacher
The Modern Mystery School

Introduction

Have you ever felt that you are not good enough? If you are human, you probably have – we have all had this experience. But for many years I thought I was the only person who felt this way. When I was young, thoughts and feelings of inadequacy were my constant companion. I did not realize that most people suffer from these limiting beliefs – usually in silence.

I have stood behind the chair as a hairdresser for over 20 years. During that time I have had many open and honest conversations with clients about feeling *less than*. I have learned that people spend a lot of time comparing themselves and their lives to others. We often think we are the only ones suffering. But in reality, we are all going through similar things.

In the beginning I just listened. I learned that every person's level of *I'm not good enough* is based on their lifetime of negative thoughts, feelings, and emotions, and how they process all the things in their lives. As I worked more closely with clients, I gained the courage to share more about my own experiences, and then the confidence to ask more questions.

When I became a board certified licensed massage therapist, I worked with the muscles, and within the energy systems of the body, and I learned more. I trained in reflexology, source point therapy, and other energy healing modalities. I learned tools that helped me clear negative energy from my body and let go of *limiting beliefs*.

Through my own personal experience, as well as the stories of my clients, I know that our thoughts, feelings, and emotions create our reality. We are not only physical beings, but also energetic beings. When we clear the energy in and around the body we can look within ourselves to heal our *limiting beliefs*. This helps us to find the happiness we truly desire, and to live the abundant, joyful life we were meant to live.

Joy and happiness are within all of us, we just need to remove what is covering them up. Living in alignment with our higher self – which is really a lot of fun – requires us to shift on a regular basis. The purpose of this book is to give you tools to help you make that shift whenever you need it. The symbols and the mantras in this book will help you move out of your head and into your heart, thereby changing your thinking and changing your experience.

How to Use This Book

This book is meant to be used like a manual. It is a book of symbols that can help you navigate through negative thoughts, feelings, and emotions that can create self-doubt, and leave you feeling completely alone, defeated, and unworthy.

I believe these symbols were gifted to me from a Higher Power to share with you. Their purpose is to help make the world a better place for us in the present moment and for all who come after us. I hope that you will enjoy them and use them for your highest good, and the highest good of all.

I have included the story of my journey to help you understand how the symbols came to be. You will read about my little shelter dog, who was the reason I dove into the field of energy work. Through her healing, I was able to heal myself as well, and then pay it forward to help others.

May you find within these pages support and inspiration for your own journey of deeper healing. I hope in sharing my story and these symbols, I can contribute to the healing of the world. This book is meant to support us as we work together toward a planet of *peace and love.*

Chapter 1

A Search for Answers

Most of us experience worry and fear, and it stops us from living our best lives. This was my story for many years, and maybe it is your story as well. What are you worried about right now? Take a few moments to make a list – maybe even write it down.

Before I learned to use symbols and mantras, I lived in a constant state of worry and fear. I worried about what I said and what I did and about what others thought of me. During my childhood I often heard, "But what will people think?" Do you remember hearing this?

Statements like these were probably not meant to stay with us for life, but in reality that is exactly what happened. They planted a seed of concern within us about what others think. Of course, this can be useful in some situations. However, since we have no real control over what others think, it can also be a waste of time and energy.

I used to worry about pretty much everything on the planet. Have you ever experienced this? I wanted to be prepared for any situation, so I would make up

scenarios in my head and envision how I would handle each one. Then I would spend hours in my head rehearsing those scenarios and planning my reaction to each. This was a total waste of time and energy, because most of the time things did not happen how I had imagined they would. But at the time, I was not aware that this was even a problem.

The worry and fear of my childhood followed me through my school years, into my adult life, and then eventually into my work life. I had so much nervous energy that I could not sit still. I was always shaking some part of my body – always on the go. Somewhere along the way, my body began to respond in negative ways to all the worry and fear in my mind. I could not sleep at night and would wake up exhausted. I fueled myself with coffee, cigarettes, and junk food, and numbed myself with alcohol. Does this sound familiar? My mind and body deteriorated from living in that constant state of high anxiety.

I was never diagnosed with anxiety, but I am pretty sure I would have been, along with ADHD and depression, had I seen a doctor. That doctor probably would have said, "Girl, you definitely need some medication." But I had no idea that what I was experiencing was not normal or that it could be changed. I just assumed that was how I was wired. And of course at that time, I would never have talked to anyone about all the thoughts in my head and how they made me feel. Because, well . . . *What would people think?*

Massage School

I began to understand my anxiety when I went to massage school. I had experienced the relaxation of receiving massage, and I decided to become a massage therapist to help others. In massage school, I learned about the nervous system; and I began to see how I was creating a state of anxiety for myself.

So how does this work? Well, there are two parts to the nervous system. One allows your body to rest and digest, the other helps you to prepare for fight or flight. The parasympathetic nervous system kicks in when your body is at rest or digesting food. It helps the body repair and recharge by letting go of the stressors. This is your body and mind at peace. It is called homeostasis or balance in the body, which is where we should ideally spend most of our time. It is considered the still point and where healing can happen in the body.

The sympathetic nervous system kicks in when we are in danger and it sends messages to the muscles that prepare them to freeze, fight or flee. The body cannot tell the difference between real physical danger or something created by the mind. The body will react in the same way to both situations. It is not healthy to live more in the sympathetic (reactive) system on a regular basis. Unfortunately, my body had learned to live in the sympathetic (fight or flight) system 24/7 and so my parasympathetic system (the rest and digest system) was not able to do its job.

Living constantly in the sympathetic system causes the body to release hormones like cortisol to help deal with the stress and prepare to take action. To release the stress hormones, the body has to have a physical outlet of movement (like running away). Without an outlet, the buildup of stress hormones in the body can cause health issues. For me, this manifested as digestive issues, exhaustion, and weight gain.

In my 20s I began to realize how much I disliked the way I felt about myself. I knew deep within me that something had to change, so I started reading self-help books. These books began the process of my seeing things differently, and I realized that I had a choice. I did not have to live in a constant state of worry and fear. They took me into a time of deeper learning, and on a powerful journey as I searched for ways to help myself. My daily goal became to feel good – feel calm – and find peace and happiness. I tried out many things, and then started to share them with others to help them as well.

Feeling What Others Feel

Through studying, reading books, and taking a lot of classes, I learned that I am an empath. What does that even mean? It means that I am a sensitive person who can pick up on all the emotions, feelings, and energies of the people around me. I actually feel what they feel. If they are sad, I feel it. If they are hurting, I feel it. If they are happy, I feel it. Looking back, I am pretty sure I was picking up energy from others my whole life, and I had no idea what was happening.

I remember sitting at a funeral feeling overwhelmed with an urge to sob loudly. I did not understand why I felt so sad when I was not even close to the person who had passed. I was just there to support a friend. Thankfully, I was able to maintain my composure until I made it out of the funeral home. I realize now that I must have been feeling the emotions of all those around me.

Through study, workshops, and classes I began to understand the blessing and the curse of being an empath. As a hairstylist, massage therapist and a healer, feeling sensitive to my clients needs can be helpful. But without a way to protect myself or release the feelings of others, being an empath had negative effects.

I believe that many people who turn to drugs, alcohol, and self-destructive behaviors are empaths looking for a way out of feeling too much. They self-medicate with drugs, alcohol and other methods to shut down, turn off, and block all the feelings they are picking up from the world around them. They do not understand what is happening, and they do not know how to protect themselves from the feelings of others.

I began to search for a solution as I came to understand how other people, as well as our own thoughts, feelings and emotions, impact us. I came to believe that if people had a way to protect themselves from the world in which they live, they would have a useful tool. The *13 Symbols* came to me when I started giving regular Reiki sessions to clients. I feel they were given to me not only to help the client on the table, but also to share with others – like you – who are looking to find inner peace and happiness. These symbols can be used by anyone. They were a gift to me, and now I am sharing them with you. Come along on the journey to discover the story of the *13 Symbols*.

Chapter 2
What Holds Us Back

One thing that holds us back from a life of joy and peace is our *limiting beliefs*. One sign that we have *limiting beliefs* is when an experience keeps recurring in our lives. For example, if we repeatedly end up in a bad relationship, we need to understand this pattern so we can heal it and break the cycle. It helps to understand where our *limiting beliefs* come from.

Limiting beliefs can come from the people around us and our interpretation of the experiences we have with those people. For example, when we were children someone might have said, "Don't be stupid." or "That was dumb." or "Why would you do something that stupid?" Then the idea of stupid enters into us. We may joke about it to give the impression it does not bother us. But each time we say it we are reinforcing the *limiting belief,* and deep inside we actually believe it. Eventually, we create more and more *limiting beliefs* that hold us back from what we want to do, be, or have.

I can recall a time when I was in grade school, I brought home my report card and I had scored a little low in one subject. My mom scolded me and told me I could do better. I think she had good intentions and believed I had higher potential. But what happened was, I felt like I was a disappointment to her. So to punish myself, I decided I would not eat my dinner. I felt like I did not deserve to eat because I had disappointed my mother. How crazy is that? But that was the level of unworthiness that I felt.

It was only one score in just one area, not the whole report card; but that one incident affected me for many years. I thought that if I did everything perfectly then I would not be a disappointment.

Limiting beliefs and negative thoughts can also come from the ego. The ego's job is to help us make good decisions so that we are safe and protected. However, it often keeps us focused on the negative as a means to keep us safe. So it brings up memories of how past experiences made us feel, to remind us that we do not want to feel that way again.

The ego remembers the time children made fun of the outfit you were wearing, or the time you unintentionally said the wrong thing and hurt someone's feelings. It remembers how it made us feel sad or unworthy. And of course, the ego always focuses on what people will think of us.

The ego is also responsible for the internal dialog that gives us anxiety, and causes us to lose sleep. It focuses on the negative, and the more negative experiences we see, the more we believe what the ego is telling us. It likes to prove that it is right, and it gives us proof through more negative experiences.

This is a vicious cycle. The ego encourages self-doubt, and we begin to believe that we are not good enough. We then start speaking to ourselves in negative ways – saying things like: *I'm an idiot, I'm so stupid, I'm such a loser.*

We have all experienced the voice inside our head. When something wonderful happens, we are on cloud nine, happy, and feeling amazing. Then, BAM, that little voice of doubt jumps in and starts to fill our minds with negative thoughts. The ego does not want us to get hurt, so it tells us that something is too good to be true or will not last. Our natural instinct is to believe that this information might be true.

We have all heard the saying that if it seems too good to be true, it probably is. So, we start to believe it. We start to question things, *hmmm maybe it is too good to be true.* Eventually, we allow that doubt to consume us, and we convince ourselves that it really must be too good to be true. Then we attract circumstances that confirm that, indeed, it was too good to be true.

The more experiences we have that follow this pattern, the more we believe what the ego is telling us. Sometimes we even self-sabotage. We start to look for reasons why it is too good to be true; we unconsciously create and attract things that make it so. We do not even realize how we are sabotaging our own happiness through our thoughts, feelings, and emotions. I was especially good at replaying scenarios over and over in my head – for *days* on end. When the thought process gets stuck in the negative it is called rumination. Have you ever done this?

The Universe Is Listening

I always say, speak kindly to yourself. Your mind, body, and spirit are listening – and so is the Universe. The Universe is always listening. When we say things out loud like, *that's just my luck, these things always happen to me, I always attract this kind of crap*, we will get more of that. The Universe is waiting and ready to send you exactly what you are speaking, thinking, and believing, because that is how powerful our words, thoughts, and beliefs are.

Another thing to consider is that the Universe cannot tell the difference between what you are creating in your mind and what is actually happening in your life. Keeping our mind focused on what we want to happen – as if it already exists – is how we attract what we really want.

We deserve to live healthy, joyous, and abundant lives. It is our Divine right. We are born with an internal knowledge of our worth; but our life experiences cause us to believe that we are not good enough, and create blocks from actually allowing the flow of good things to come to us. The programming of our lives has taught us to doubt that we are worthy. So first we have to believe that we are worthy. Then we can accept and allow the flow of good and wonderful things that will come to us.

The allowing part can be very difficult since our thought patterns have been with us for years. Some patterns we create ourselves because of our life experiences; others are created for us by the people around us, like our parents, teachers, friends, bosses, neighbors, and acquaintances. What we have to realize is this:

I AM THE MASTER OF MY UNIVERSE!
(This is a great mantra.)

Therefore, I am responsible for keeping the ego in check with positive thoughts. The universe responds by giving us positive experiences. Then we will attract more positive things into our lives because – we get what we think about.

Here is a great example. Have you ever thought *Hmm, I wonder how so and so is doing. I haven't seen her in such a long time*. And the very next day you run into her at the grocery store? It happens all of the time. This is just one small example of how we manifest what we think about. Test it out. Think about someone and see how long before you hear from them or run into them.

Now that we understand some of what holds us back, let us look at how we can shift.

Chapter 3

Shifting Our Perspective

There are many tools for shifting the mind when it is going crazy. Sometimes falling asleep can break the cycle. Meditation can calm and reset the mind. Breath awareness works to occupy the mind as we intentionally inhale and exhale. Repeating a mantra, aloud or silently, can calm the mind. And of course the symbols in this book can shift the mind. I have used all of these tools to stop the endless mind chatter. Let us take a look at some of these.

When we are spiraling down the rabbit hole of negative thought patterns the first tool to use is that of awareness. Sometimes that alone is enough to shift our experience. When doubt, fear, or negative thoughts creep in we can make a conscious effort to replace them with something positive. Sometimes it is hard, but if we do it we can receive more positive things to think about. When we shift our thinking over and over we are rewiring our brains and reprogramming our thinking. The more we stay in a positive mindset, the more we can avoid resistance in our lives.

Empowering Emotional Staircase

You can change your mental state when you change your focus. By changing the thoughts in your head you will be able to affect not only your own world, but also the world around you. One way to shift is to use The Emotional Staircase. The staircase asks you to choose a word to express how you feel at that moment and then work your way up the list, which will help shift your state of mind.

Use Emotional Staircase as a tool to help you navigate through your feelings. Look at this list. Choose a word that describes where you are right now. Then, choose a thought that carries you to the next word. How does that feel now? Continue moving up the list to a higher word and notice how your mood shifts. By climbing the staircase you are shifting your experience.

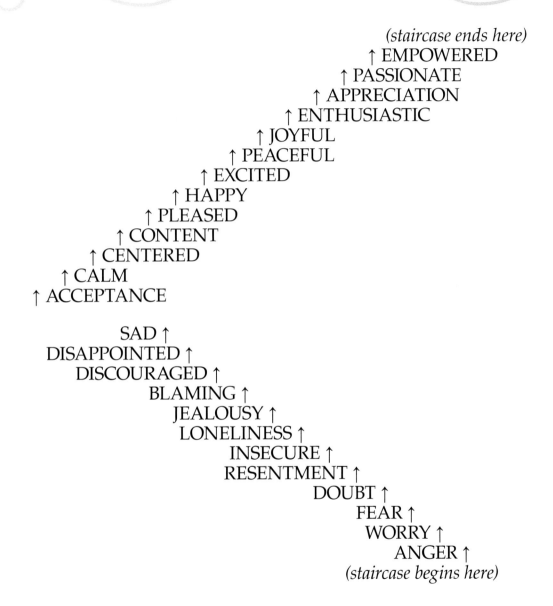

(staircase ends here)
↑ EMPOWERED
↑ PASSIONATE
↑ APPRECIATION
↑ ENTHUSIASTIC
↑ JOYFUL
↑ PEACEFUL
↑ EXCITED
↑ HAPPY
↑ PLEASED
↑ CONTENT
↑ CENTERED
↑ CALM
↑ ACCEPTANCE

SAD ↑
DISAPPOINTED ↑
DISCOURAGED ↑
BLAMING ↑
JEALOUSY ↑
LONELINESS ↑
INSECURE ↑
RESENTMENT ↑
DOUBT ↑
FEAR ↑
WORRY ↑
ANGER ↑
(staircase begins here)

Use a Mantra

Mantras are useful tools to help with this shift. I have a mantra that I use regularly to help me get out of my head. It goes like this: *I am happy. I am healthy. I am wealthy.* Feel free to borrow my mantra or create one that resonates with you. When I become aware of a negative thought pattern, I start repeating my mantra in my head. This is the easiest way to shift negative thoughts.

You cannot hold two thoughts at once, so the positive one can edge out the negative one. For example, think about chocolate chip cookies and vegetables. Your mind flips back and forth: cookies, veggies, cookies, veggies. It is impossible to think of both at the same time. It is one or the other. When you are in your head replaying the broken record and you recognize what is happening, repeat your mantra over and over. If your thoughts go back to the broken record, you recognize it, and again repeat your mantra.

Each of the 13 Symbols comes with a title that can be used as a mantra. Using the symbol and the mantra together can be a very powerful shift. When you are stuck on a thought, try using this pattern of repeating the mantra and visualizing the symbols in your head; eventually you will realize that you have not had the negative thought in your mind.

Perspective

The truth is, we are *all good enough*! We are strong enough – God gives us the strength to carry us through absolutely anything. We are smart enough – we are pretty enough or handsome enough. We are everything we were created to be. We are worthy enough!!! We have the capacity to accomplish anything we want. We are beautiful people and all things are possible for us. It is our Divine right to be *enough*. We just have to believe it – allow it – and accept it.

Surrounding yourself with people who are also on the path of progression to learn more about themselves will help support you in your growth and help move you along your path.

We are all in this together; and knowing someone else has been through what you are experiencing can help you find the courage and strength to make it through the tough times. Having tools like the 13 Symbols can help you in that moment to rise above whatever is happening at that time. You can simply choose a tool and use it to work your way out of your current state of negativity in order to change your focus and shift your mindset.

As we talked about in Chapter 2, most of our lives are spent with other people (parents, teachers, friends, etc) layering on us their thoughts, feelings, emotions, concerns and opinions. It is up to us to seek tools that help peel back all those layers. Only then can we refill that empty space to internalize healthier feelings and thoughts. This will gradually reprogram our negative thinking.

The more we learn – and practice what we learn – the better we become at finding tools to help ourselves. We all have the *knowing* deep inside – we know that we are meant to live an abundant, healthy, happy life. We just have to continually remind ourselves, and self-advocate to help move ourselves toward a happier – and hopefully, more joyful – state of mind.

Chapter 4

A Whole New World

One of the most profound shifts in my life happened when I discovered energy work. In my early twenties, after years of living in a state of constant stress, I began searching for happiness and inner peace. As I said before, I was a nervous and anxious person. I was in a constant state of worry and fear. I was always ready for whatever might happen, whether it was standing and fighting, or running and hiding. The sympathetic nervous system was running my life. As a result, my breathing was extremely shallow, and my heart was usually racing. I had such a nervous stomach, you could see it under my shirt jumping like it had its very own heartbeat. I was a mess.

When I was in school, I worked hard to prove to the teachers that: I deserved to be taught; was smart enough; that I deserved and desired the education and knowledge they had to offer. I felt like everyone around me believed I did not even deserve their time. I did not feel like I deserved it, so I thought that the teachers felt the same way.

I know now this was just my young mind's interpretation that came from feeling like I was not good enough. In reality, I had no way of knowing what other people were thinking. It was just what I *thought* they were thinking. This was my ego guiding me. All that speculation did nothing but make me a nervous wreck, leaving me with anxiety and depression.

I love learning and I would pour myself into whatever I was studying. Once I became aware that I was in a constant state of anxiety, I began the search for a way to calm myself. My journey to health began with the self-help books that I mentioned earlier.

I began reading and learning, and gained knowledge of: how the energy in and around the body works; what foods would make me feel alive; how exercising and moving the body increases health; and how essential oils and herbs can be used to calm the mind. It was a whole new world!

Most importantly, I learned about self-talk, and how this can affect us on many levels. Internal self-talk can have a negative or a positive effect on us. Our mind's default is negative self-talk. I recall a time when as a manager I had given an employee many days off. Every time she asked for a day off I gave it to her. Then one time I had to say 'no'. When I told her she could not have that one off, she yelled at me, "You never give me days off. You always give everyone else days off, but not me." From my point of view I only said 'no' one time. But from her perspective, with a brain trained to focus on the negative, the situation looked and felt very different for her.

This is what the ego does. It clouds our perspective. This employee could not see all the times when things worked out in her favor. She could only focus on the one time it did not. This is how the brain and the ego run our lives. For many years

I let the ego run my life – creating worry, fear and anxiety, which created many physical ailments. This was a terrible state in which to exist, but I did not know how to change it. Then I discovered the world of energy healing modalities.

Everything is energy, and the energy vibrates at different speeds and frequencies. As beings in this world we can learn to shift our vibration to help us match the speed and frequency of the things we desire. I have learned that there are usually some *limiting beliefs* deep within us that hold us back.

I learned about creating an energy ball and giving that energy to myself. I discovered meditation to help calm the mind. I learned about meridian channels through which the energy of the body flows. I learned about the aura, which is like an energetic skin.

On this journey into a whole new world I had a wonderful teacher, and her name was Little Bitt. Hers is a most amazing story.

Chapter 5

The Little Teacher

Help, training, and teachers often come at the most unlikely times, and from the most unlikely places. I found my next teacher in an animal shelter.

I have always enjoyed helping out at the local shelter – it helped calm the thoughts in my head and forget about my own issues for a little while. Spending time with animals can be a wonderful way to shift ourselves. At the local shelter, I worked mostly with dogs. I would take them for walks, and shower them with lots of love. A shelter can be a high stress situation for some animals, and showing them some love helped bring joy to my heart.

One day, a little dog came into the shelter who was terrified. She was pregnant with a litter full of puppies and she had a spinal injury. The spinal injury made it so she could not hold her bladder or her bowels. Her back end dragged when she walked. She was so scared that she growled or barked when I tried to come close. She just did not trust people, so she kept them at a distance.

Her life experiences had created a situation where she felt like she had to protect herself. Her reaction was the same as it would be for a person who had experienced trauma. We are wired to do whatever it takes to keep ourselves safe. That is exactly what this little dog was trying to do.

This, of course, made it very difficult to clean her kennel. When I met her I pointed my finger at her, looked her right in the eyes and told her, "Listen little girl. I am going to be your best friend." I made up my mind at that moment that I was going to do whatever it took to get her to trust me. And so I bribed her with chicken.

They say the way to a man's heart is through his stomach. I figured if it works for people it could work for a dog as well. At first, she would not take the chicken. She would look at it, then look at me, as if to say, "No chance, lady."

One day, I layed on the floor with my arm under her kennel and put the chicken on my finger. She would not take the chicken. I stopped throughout the day to check on her and offer her some chicken. She would look at me then look at the chicken on my finger, then look at me again, but she would not take it from me. If I laid the chicken down and looked away, she would eat it.

On the third day, she reluctantly took the food from my finger. She began to trust me and let me touch her, then pet her, and eventually hold her. I always cheer for the underdog (pun intended). I believe there is good in everyone, and everyone deserves to be loved. I knew in my heart that this little dog was a good dog. I knew deep inside of me that she just needed someone to love her. I took the time to gain her trust, and let her get to know me, and that is how our bond began.

After she had her puppies and they were all adopted, I took her to a local vet who did acupuncture and he prescribed herbs for her. She would return to the shelter and would do well for a day or so, then go back to her old self – growling, showing her teeth, and barking at anyone who came near her kennel.

How do you try to protect yourself? For me, I shut down, go within, and distance myself. This little dog could not remove herself from her situation so she protected herself with aggression. I decided that maybe a different environment would help her so I fostered her. I brought her home and called her Little Bitt. My husband, Rick, was thrilled when I brought her home. Since Little Bitt did not care for men, it was a little tricky in the beginning.

When I got her home I did everything I could to help her feel calm and safe. I played relaxing music, diffused essential oils near her kennel, and even put crystals under her bedding. Every night after work Little Bitt would come to me and I would pick her up. She would lay on my chest all wrapped up in a blanket and I would just hold her.

I did not know much about energy work at that time, but decided I would try to do something for her. I knew that energy follows intention. So I would place my fingers along either side of her spine in the area where I thought she was injured and set the intention to send her love and healing energy.

Immediately I felt a strong pulsing in my fingers. Holding my hands on her injury, I repeated, "I send you loving, healing energy." I thought: *All things thrive with love.* I envisioned our hearts connected with a stream of green, healing light. I shared *all* the love in my heart with her. Every night she would come to me, and I would pick her up and we would repeat the whole process. We often fell asleep with her in my arms.

We worked together in these sessions for months and months. As the sessions continued, I noticed tremendous improvements in her. Little Bitt learned to go up and down the stairs. She would put her front paws up on my leg and stand up. Eventually, she was able to stand briefly on her hind legs. She became stronger and more playful. She even started to trust my husband and began to run a little. She became so strong and confident – and now she can run as if she were not handicapped.

One night, she came and I held out my hands and asked, "Do you want me to hold you baby?" She looked at me for a second and turned and walked away. I feel at that moment she made the decision that she was OK. I was so sad, and yet so happy that she had reached the point where she felt safe and did not need me as much. I was excited that the work we had done had helped her heal.

The plan was to help her heal so she could be adopted. But, through working with her, I fell in love. To me, Little Bitt was such a special dog. I could not bear the thought of her ending up in an environment where someone might be unkind to her. So, I adopted her, making a commitment to her that I would always protect her to the best of my ability.

Little Bitt is a very sweet, loving little dog. When I look at her now, my heart is filled with an abundance of love and joy. She gets to be herself and has blossomed into this amazing dog simply because I did not give up on her. I gave her an opportunity to see that things could be different than what life had shown her. I am so proud of her for taking a chance and trusting me. She is very protective of me and even protects me from my husband. She has come to trust him, but since I am her person she will get between us and bark at him. It is like she is saying, "Hey that's my person. Don't mess with her." I think because I gave her a chance, she is committed to protecting me as much as I am committed to protecting her.

It is no coincidence that our paths crossed. This little girl had a lesson for me about unconditional love and above all, self-love. Self-love is something with which I have always struggled – and I think many of us do because we do not feel good enough. Little Bitt taught me that there is no need for us to try to be someone that we are not. It is our Divine right to love and be loved.

I believe that Little Bitt made a choice the day she took the chicken from my finger. She chose to trust and accept my love, and that decision changed her life. This is a powerful lesson for us all. We have the ability to change our lives. We just have to decide we want things to be different, then take action to pursue a path that helps us achieve what we desire.

I was so thrilled that Little Bitt was transformed from my love and the energy work. I thought to myself, *Wow, if energy work can have this kind of result, then I have to learn more about it!*

Little Bitt, my first teacher of energy work

Chapter 6

Discovering the Symbols

I began reading books about Reiki – and learned that Reiki is energy healing that uses symbols to increase the power of the energy. This is God energy or Universal Life Force energy. We all have the energy within us, we just need to tap into and develop our connection to it.

This Universal Life Force energy has an intelligence of its own and goes into the body where it is needed. It helps us to peel away layers of mental-emotional stuff and negative energies that have been building in our energy field since before we were born – things that were planted in our minds by other's comments, beliefs, and fears. This negative energy that surrounds us holds us back from what we truly want. These negative energies also feed the ego.

I found a Reiki Master near me and began my Reiki journey. I became a Reiki Master myself in the Usiu System of Reiki. I started sharing Little Bitt's story – how I used Reiki to help her and how much she had improved. When I first became a Reiki Master, I felt like I could not offer it as a service because I did not think I was good enough, or knew enough, or had enough experience. The truth is, I had everything I needed except the confidence to know that I had everything I needed.

Over time I became more and more confident. I continued to study Reiki and its benefits. I found that I loved Reiki and when I talked about it my passion came through, and a lot of people were willing to give it a try. People started asking me to teach it to them so they could learn to do it for themselves and their families. As the saying goes, when the teacher is ready the student appears, and when the student is ready the teacher appears. So, I created courses and taught my interpretation of the information I had gathered through my studies. I have been blessed to share my interpretation of the Life Force energy with many people.

In my role as a massage therapist I could see myself combining energy work with what I was already doing in order to bring another level of healing to my clients.

When I learned about Reiki we were taught to draw the symbols a few different ways. One way was to trace the symbol in our mind with the nose leading with a slight movement of the head. I realized right away that I had traced things like this my entire life. I would visually trace the outline of someone's face while they were talking to me. I would draw their eyes, and their nose, and their mouth, and their ears. I would outline a stop sign or any object that caught my eye. So drawing the symbols made perfect sense and seemed very natural.

As I did Reiki sessions with clients, my head would start moving in different ways, and I would just go with it. Then I would realize I was drawing a symbol. It was a symbol I did not recognize, nor did I have a name for it. I would use the symbol throughout the session, not knowing why I was using it or the meaning of it. Reiki relies heavily on listening to your guides and following your intuition. I was taught that if you receive a symbol, it is yours and you should use it.

Then in meditation, I would ask for information about the symbol and I would get a name for it. The names pretty much explained why I received and used a particular symbol. I kept the symbols in a notebook to refer back to later. I wrote the date each symbol was revealed to me; and when I got the name I wrote it along side the symbol in the notebook. I had no idea why I was even writing them down, but something told me I needed to record them.

Later, when I had all the symbols, I knew why I was recording them – it was so I could put them into a book to share with others how they could use them to improve their lives.

As I was recording the symbols, I noticed a pattern was starting to develop. There were times when I felt like my client would have more benefit from the session if I had a symbol for whatever issue was a struggle for them – and I would ask for one.

There were times when I would see the full symbol, and I would just know its purpose and how to draw it. Other times my head would start moving, tracing whatever my mind was revealing. Then later, I would record the

symbol – sometimes receiving the name right away, other times the name would come much later.

In Reiki, the names of the symbols are considered their mantras. You draw the symbol once and say the mantra three times. That is how I use these symbols, whether for myself or for my clients.

The more I practiced Reiki, the more symbols I received. Over the next year, I received 13 symbols. I feel I have been called to share these symbols with everyone who needs them. I feel that these symbols were given to me to share as a reminder to us that we are *all enough – good enough – pretty enough – handsome enough – strong enough*. **We are Enough**. Because that is how we were created.

The 13 Symbols were given to me to share with you, so you can identify and release the limiting beliefs and patterns that hold you back from the life you want to live. Together, we can elevate our existence here on this planet.

Chapter 7

The 13 Symbols

Have you ever considered the energy that symbols carry? Look at the Nike, Apple, or Pepsi symbols – each carries its own energy. When you see the symbols of these companies and many others, it sends a message to the brain. This is powerful. Hundreds of years ago, when most people did not read or write, symbols guided them. Stores, pubs and businesses were identified by a symbol. Imagine that world.

The 13 Symbols are a powerful tool. As you work with the 13 Symbols in this book you will come to recognize them as symbols to help shift your mindset. You can use them to shift your thoughts in order to shift how you feel. Use them, enjoy them, and make them a part of your everyday life.

You can draw the symbols with pen and paper or with your finger. Follow the arrows to draw the symbol. The name of the symbols can be used as a mantra to interrupt negative thought patterns. Say the name or mantra three times (or more if you feel called) as repeating the mantras can help elevate your mood. This gives power to your intention.

1. Release and Let Go

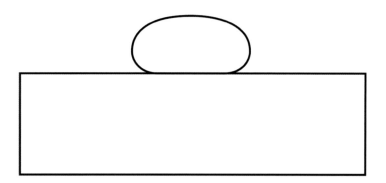

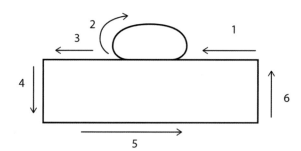

Use **Release and Let Go** to release and let go of something.

This symbol helps you release and let go of:

- Things that no longer serve you
- Anything that keeps you from being happy
- Limiting beliefs that hold you back
- Everything that does not serve your higher purpose

Follow the flow of the arrows with your finger or a paper and pen.

2. Move Mountains

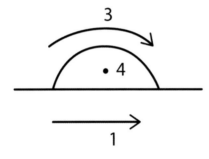

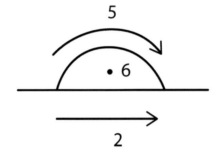

Use **Move Mountains** to assist you in releasing the really BIG things:

- Thoughts, feelings and emotions that have been with you for a long time
- Things that seem impossible to release
- Fears, ideas, and limiting beliefs that feel like they are a part of you
- Things that are blocking you from receiving what you want

I encourage you to use this symbol to help Move your Mountains!

3. Receive Healing

You are worthy and you deserve to live in a healthy body.

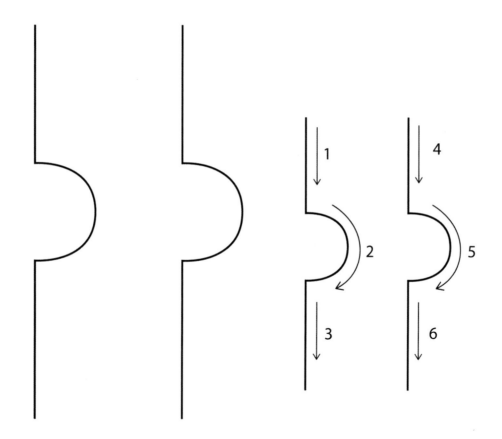

Use **Receive Healing** to allow the healing energy to flow – to help yourself heal on all levels.

These questions may help you discover places that you can receive healing (by using this symbol):

- Are you holding a loved one's pain for him or her?
- What parts of you feel unworthy and can receive healing?
- What part of you does not feel worthy of healing?
- Is there a part of you that wants to suffer?
- Do you carry a belief about disease or illness that exists in your family line?

Awareness will help you find the places that need healing.

4. Positive Energy Spiral

We do not get to choose what happens to us. However, we do get to choose how we respond. When something happens, we need to reconnect to the Universe to find the power of positive energy.

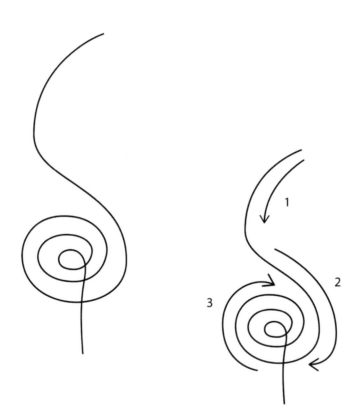

Use **Positive Energy Spiral** to fill the empty space created by letting go and releasing, so that the negative does not reclaim that space. Positive energy, full of love and light, will spiral through and serve this purpose well.

Use **Positive Energy Spiral** when you:

- Are anxious, nervous or worried
- Feel like someone is sucking the life out of you
- Are depressed
- Wish to change your focus
- Want to protect yourself from toxic situations or people

5. I Am Enough!

Our experiences guide our thoughts, which guide our feelings, which in turn guide our emotions. The emotions then guide our actions. When the pattern is stuck in the negative, the I'm not good enough feeling arises. When we allow it to take hold we beat ourselves up in unhealthy ways, and choose destructive behaviors.

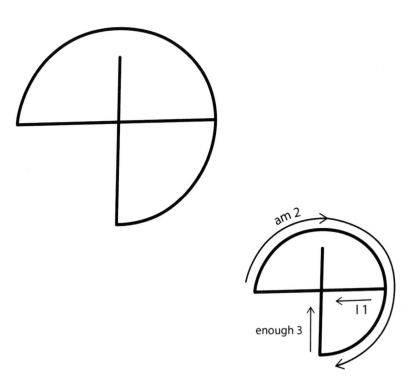

Use I Am Enough All Day, Every Day!

As I shared earlier, every person suffers from the feeling that *I am not good enough* – so everyone can benefit from using this symbol.

Use **I Am Enough** when you:

- Are struggling to believe in yourself
- Are replaying something repeatedly in your head
- Want to raise your confidence
- Need a boost

Use this symbol to believe in yourself! *You are Enough!* We are divine creatures of the Universe created by God. We are here to experience ALL the good and wonderful things the Universe has to offer.

6. Be One with the Universe

Being One with the Universe means we are in alignment with our true purpose as humans.

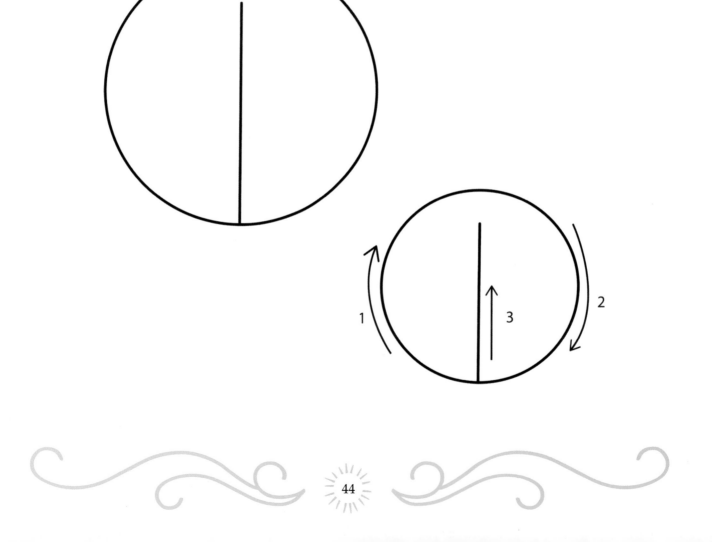

Use **At One with the Universe** to reconnect to the power of the universe and your true purpose.

This symbol works with the next one: Universal Connection.

7. Universal Connection

This is a way to understand connection to the Divine or Source.

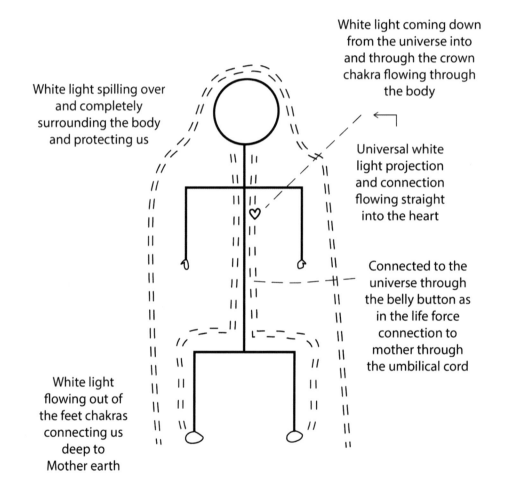

White light coming down from the universe into and through the crown chakra flowing through the body

White light spilling over and completely surrounding the body and protecting us

Universal white light projection and connection flowing straight into the heart

Connected to the universe through the belly button as in the life force connection to mother through the umbilical cord

White light flowing out of the feet chakras connecting us deep to Mother earth

Use **Universal Connection** when you need to remind yourself of your connection to source.

Envision a green light (the color of the heart chakra) coming down from source straight into your heart.

Envision a white light running up your central core from your solar plexus (above your belly button) up to the source.

See yourself surrounded in white light, and know you carry that light with you.

Note: I first connected with the green light of the heart when I was working with Little Bitt's heart Chakra. Chakras are spinning wheels of energy and light that connect our physical body to our spiritual body and vibrate out into the Universe.

The Chakras are part of our energy field and are impacted by how we interact with those around us.

8. Align and Balance

It is possible to have all that you desire. When you are perfectly aligned and balanced, you feel joy and it is easy to stay focused. Sometimes your life experiences pull you out of balance making it difficult to remain positive and happy. Negative thoughts can be much more powerful than the positive ones. When the negative thoughts grab hold, focus on the Align and Balance symbol.

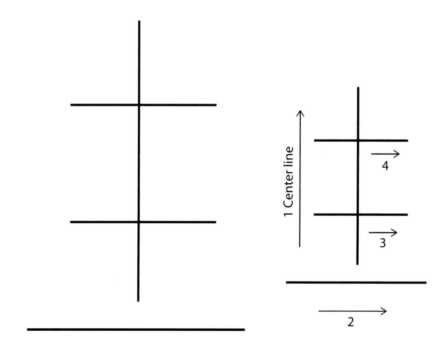

This will help remind you that we are all connected. We are all part of the Collective Consciousness and the vast Universe. We can be at one with the Universe.

Use **Align and Balance** to become aligned and balanced with what you truly desire.

- Close your eyes and envision the light connection to Divine Source, through your heart and belly button.
- Know that you are safe and protected – the Universe has your back.
- You are aligned, balanced, and vibrating at the same speed and frequency as what you desire.
- You are supported by the Collective in this alignment.

9. Joy

When you use Release and Let Go to clear something, a great follow up is the symbol for Joy. It is simple and easy to fill the empty space with the symbol of Joy.

Use **Joy** to:

- Find moments of Joy throughout your day
- Celebrate the things that make you happy
- Shift your focus from negative thoughts

The more you practice moments of Joy the more moments you will find to enjoy. Remember, we get what we think about. If you are full of Joy, gratitude and positive energy there is no room for the negative.

Fill yourself, your mind, your heart, your soul, with pure **Joy**.

10. Stand In Your Power

We are powerful beings created by a higher power. We have everything we need to live the vibrant life we desire already inside of us. It is easy to let others influence how we feel and think. You will feel this in your gut (your solar plexus, which is your powerhouse). This is when you need to stand in your power.

Use **Stand In Your Power** when:

- It feels like someone just punched you in the gut
- You have feelings of dread
- It feels like the life was sucked out of you
- You feel powerless
- You want to take back your power

11. Divinely Guided and Protected

This is a symbol representing the flow of Divine Guidance.

I am Devinely Guided,
Protected and connected

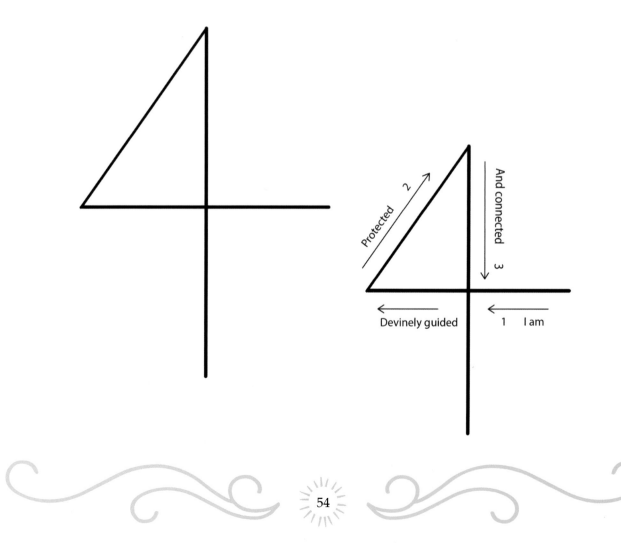

Use **Divinely Guided and Protected** when you:

- Need clarity or guidance
- Need a little extra protection
- Go to sleep at nighttime
- Wake up in the morning

This grounds in a lighter energy to the earth (where we physically exist) allowing us to connect with divine energy.

12. **I Am Grateful**

This symbol came to me later than the others did. It feels like a reminder to be grateful for all the good and wonderful things we have in our lives. You can think of this symbol as a fancy check. Keep gratitude on your to-do list and check it off each day.

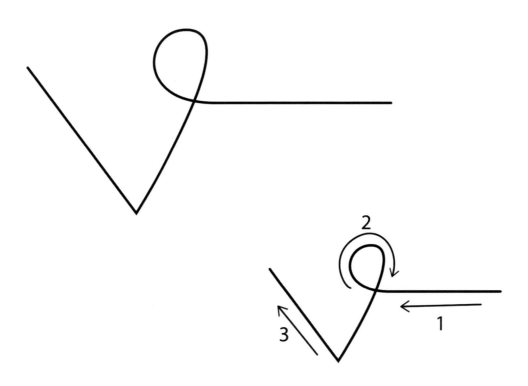

Use **I Am Grateful** when you:

- Wake up in the morning
- Go to sleep at night
- Notice amazing things
- Are with family and friends

When you live in gratitude the Universe gives you more things to be grateful for. A gratitude journal is another tool you can incorporate in your daily practice.

13. Courage and Strength

Sometimes we have to go through hard things, but know that you can turn to this symbol for support.

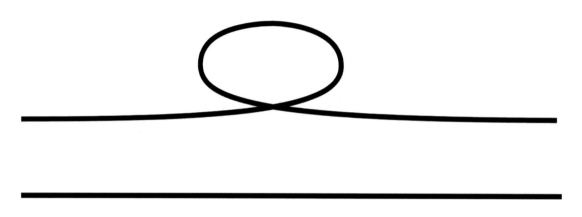

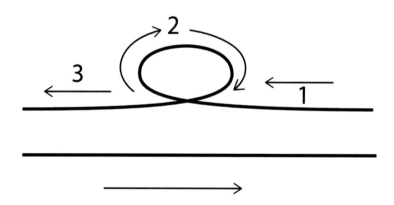

Use **Courage and Strength** when:

- You find yourself in a tough situation
- You need a reminder that you are a powerful being
- Life seems like a struggle

The tough times will seem easier when you use this symbol to empower you with more courage and strength.

The 13 Symbols

1. Release and Let Go
2. Move Mountains
3. Receive Healing
4. Positive Energy Spiral
5. I Am Enough!
6. Be One with the Universe
7. Universal Connection
8. Align and Balance
9. Joy
10. Stand in your Power
11. Divinely Guided and Protected
12. I Am Grateful
13. Courage and Strength

You Are Your Superpower

I give you these symbols to help you **Shift** whenever you want to shift. I give you these symbols so that you can: release, heal, align, find guidance, and live with courage and joy as you stand in your power. I hope that you can take these symbols and use them to help make your life easier. Use them to help yourself and others on the spiritual journey of coming to **Know Thyself.** Honor what makes you uniquely you and live as the most you that you can be. Be strong. Be Powerful. Be Authentic. Live your life to the fullest and enjoy every moment.

I use these symbols to help me move through my lessons, through uncomfortable situations, and for clearing energetic space, so that I can move into Love and Happiness. I even used the symbols to help me write the book. I started receiving the symbols in 2015. I wanted to share them with the world to help others as the symbols had helped me. So, I bought a book publishing package in 2018, thinking it would motivate me to finish this book.

Then my own limiting beliefs, fears, and doubts caused me to struggle to finish this project. I battled with thoughts of unworthiness when I tried to write and kept telling myself I was not a writer. But I am a storyteller with personal life experiences to share. I used the 13 Symbols to overcome my fears, and with the

help of the Universal powers, here we are. It took years, but I know that everything happens in Divine timing.

Something was calling me and thankfully I listened. When something is calling you, Listen! It may be a sign that what you have to offer the world is You! You are your superpower.

The Universe will support you on your journey.

You are divinely guided and protected, always.

Much Love and Happy Healing from me to you!

♡ Lena

Glossary of Terms

Chakra – spinning wheel of energy located throughout the body

Limiting belief – a belief that reflects this is how things are and they can not be changed. *Limiting beliefs* are put on us by the people in our lives, our environment, and our experiences

Reflexologist – one who works with techniques that target specific reflex points in the body that correspond with the organs of the body

Source Point Therapy – a healing modality that focuses on scanning the body for imbalances in the energy field, then bringing in the energy of the blueprint of Health back to the body

Suggested Reading List

The Biology of Belief, Bruce H. Lipton, PhD

The Amazing Power of Deliberate Intent, Esther and Jerry Hicks

Manifesting Change, Mike Dooley

Change the Story of Your Health, Carl Greer, PhD, PsyD

How to Heal Yourself When No One Else Can, Amy B. Scher

You Can Heal Your Life, Louise Hay

Daily Positive Affirmations, Louise Hay

Energy Healing for Women, Keith Sherwood and Sabine Wittmann

The Tapping Solution, Nick Ortner

Your Body Speaks Your Mind, Deb Shapiro

The Healing Code, Alexander Loyd, PhD, ND with Ben Johnson, MD, DO, NMD

10 Secrets for Success and Inner Peace, Dr. Wayne W. Dyer

Being In Balance, Dr. Wayne W. Dyer

Ascend to Joy, Christine Elwart

Acknowledgments

I want to give a *huge* shoutout for the help and guidance of some very significant people. I am so grateful for their guidance in this process. I do not think I could have finished this without you.

Christine Elwart, an amazing Guide, Healer, Teacher, and Author of *Ascend to Joy.* Thank you for the connection to Heather Davis Desrocher, and for always being there to answer questions and guide me along my path.

Heather Davis Desrocher, my editor and the author of *Manuscript Magic, 7 Simple Steps to Writing a Book.* Your guidance was instrumental in the completion of this book. *Manuscript Magic* was my reference manual to finding within me what needed to be shared. Thank you for believing in me and helping me complete this project.

To those at Balboa Press who continually checked in on me to see how my project was moving along: Thank you for all the time spent reaching out and reminding me to finish what I started.

To my precious Tiny Bitt, I am forever grateful you came into my life. I love you unconditionally with all my heart.

To my husband, thank you for letting me be me, never trying to change me, and always encouraging me.

And last but not least, my family. I would not be who I am today without you. Each of you have played a significant role in shaping who I am. With your encouragement, your belief, and your support, I have grown in so many ways. Thank you to each and every one of you!

About the Author

Lena has devoted her life to learning, growing, and evolving so she can empower herself and others. She is a licensed cosmetologist, board certified licensed massage therapist, certified Life Activation Practitioner, healer, and teacher. Lena seeks practical tools to live a life full of health and joy for herself and others.

When Lena began to study with the Modern Mystery School, her life changed drastically. She became a certified Life Activation Practitioner, Ensofic Ray Practitioner, a teacher, and a healer. This training allows her to use many healing modalities to clear and balance energies of and around the body so that her clients can feel great and live in joy.

Lena lives in Wapakoneta, Ohio, with her husband and three rescue dogs, including Little Bitt. If you would like to find out how Lena's services can help you on your journey of health and wellness, contact her at shiftwithsymbols.com

Connect with Lena at www.energeticconnection.net
Facebook: Shift with Symbols
Email: shiftwithsymbols@gmail.com

Printed in the United States
by Baker & Taylor Publisher Services